CW00816079

Valeria Shashenok

Things that just make sense in a bomb shelter

story.one – Life is a story

 story.one

1st edition 2022
© story.one – the library of life – www.story.one
A brand of Storylution GmbH

Font set from Minion Pro and Lato.

Editor English Text: David Granger

© Photos: Valeria Shashenok
Contact: valerisssh@story.one

ISBN: 978-3-903715-25-7

This is not a film. This is real life.
Or how life can change.

CONTENT

Dedication

My name's Valeria Shashenok. I'm 20 years-old and I come from Chernihiv, just outside of Kyiv in the north of Ukraine.

I'm a freelance photographer and used to use my social accounts – mostly TikTok and Instagram – to show my work to clients.

Then, when Putin decided to invade Ukraine in February 2022, I filmed and photographed what was going on, what I saw, and posted it on these accounts. For one of these posts, I remembered a TikTok trend I'd seen:

"Things that just make sense in …"

For me, at that time, it was "Things that just make sense in a bomb shelter …" because that's where I was living with my mother and father: in a bomb shelter. Since that video was posted, many things have changed. I was no longer simply filming and documenting events in my city to show the world what was happening in

Ukraine, now I'd became part of the media coverage: I was interviewed by CNN and on the BBC – and because of this, suddenly I began to get millions of views on my own channels.

The stories I was interviewed about were how I escaped in cars, trains and buses from the Ukrainian city of Chernihiv to Warsaw in Poland then Berlin in Germany before finally ending up in Milan. I had travelled to Italy before the war – I love the country. It was one of the pictures on my "Map of Dreams" I had in my flat which I put together to map out what I wanted to achieve and do. On it there were pictures of different things ... of Italy and Scrooge McDuck diving into a pile of money.

But it wasn't all TikTok trends and funny films during my escape from Ukraine.

On 30 March 2022, I posted a story about my cousin who was like a brother to me. He was killed by a Russian bomb. On this post, there were three pictures and in the caption I said it was Putin who had killed my cousin. I want everyone to know what has happened to me. Because, for me, this war is a terrible reality.

I posted the story about my cousin at 10pm and within 24 hours it was seen by a lot of people. But people seeing the post and knowing the story of my cousin doesn't change anything – it won't change the fact he was killed by a Russian bomb.

This book is not dedicated to my cousin. And it's not dedicated to my mom or my dad (both of whom are still in Ukraine) or to the people of Chernihiv or to all those who have been killed during the invasion.

Actually, I want to dedicate these stories to the Russian people. Because many people in Russia still don't believe that this is a war against Ukraine, but a "special operation". But in a special operation, Russian soldiers wouldn't use this level of violence, destroy houses, shave women's heads or abuse children.

February 24

February 24 was the day war started, the day it all really began for me.

My mom came into my room and said: "Valeria – there's been a bomb in Kyiv and destroyed buildings." I actually live in my flat in the Ukrainian capital city of Kyiv, but a few days before February 24, I had travelled to Chernihiv, back to be with my parents to the home they lived in and I grew up in.

Our flat in Chernihiv, where I grew up, is the best place in the world. It's full of memories and emotions. I experienced all the ups and downs of my childhood there. It's an apartment with high ceilings and big windows and I love it when the wooden floor creaks when I enter my bedroom. I like it when I come into the kitchen and my mother is cooking – it's really cosy, really comforting.

This flat, this place, takes me back to when I was a child. I am the youngest in the family which means I will always remain the little girl to everyone. The school I went to is close to our house and I had a wonderful time there – even though all the teachers hated me (!).

That morning, February 24, it was a very strange feeling when my mom woke me up. The first thing I wanted to know was which buildings had been bombed and where, so I turned on my phone to check if my friends had written anything in our Telegram group. Telegram is the app where we discuss everything.

My friends told me the war had started. One of them, my friend Aksinia had tried to get to the Czech Republic that day to see her boyfriend. When she arrived at the airport, it was closed – landmines had been scattered across the runway. She was really upset. She said everyone had run out of the airport, afraid. She was the first person I knew who had seen or witnessed the situation. It is horrific when you hear bombs. You can hear them, but you can't do anything about it – you're just a toy.

It was 24 February and the sky was grey when Putin invaded, when the explosions started in Kyiv – the ones my mom woke me to tell me about.

I had breakfast that morning and went outside to see what the situation in Chernihiv was like. I had never expected anything would actually happen.

When I went outside I saw long queues everywhere, people were queuing to get cash out of the ATMs. The first thing my father did, as the war started, was go and buy fuel.

I filmed Ukrainian soldiers with my cellphone, until they came over and asked me to delete the videos and the photos. I was shooting on my phone because I was scared to take out my camera. I'd spent a lot of money on a new camera, specifically to take pictures in Kyiv. But I was now afraid to take it with me – the Ukrainian soldiers didn't want to be filmed anyway. It was really frightening.

But still, despite everything, I didn't think there would be a war, that the war would actually start. A lot of people were talking about when they thought it would begin. I had a friend who had already left, who escaped to the east, who told me the war would start one day soon. But it seemed like everyone talked about the war starting, but no-one believed it. Or no-one wanted to believe it.

" My mother is always up for anything. I said: Mum, dance a little. And she just did, grabbed a yellow plastic toolbox and danced around the bunker with it. "

"Things That Just Make Sense in a Bomb Shelter"

The war really had started.

On 26 February, a Saturday morning, I woke up. Well, to be honest, my dog Torry woke me up. I saw my mother kept going over to the windows of our flat to see what was happening outside. She said: "Lera, look! There's a soldier," and, when I did look, I could see he was really heavily armed. A Ukrainian soldier right in front of our flat and he's got three or four different weapons on him.

People were already out supporting the soldiers, bringing them bread and food.

I looked at this soldier and to me it didn't matter if he was outside our house or not, but my mom was very, very nervous. She said to my father: "We should really drive to the bomb shelter, come on." But my dad replied (relaxed as ever): "Calm down. Why does it bother you?" Only half an hour later though, he said: "Lera, get yourself ready, we're going to the bomb shelter." I asked: "Why? Why should we go?" I wanted to go back to sleep, because it was early – for me – about 9 am. Then everything happened really quickly. By 10 am we were already in the bomb shelter.

Our shelter had been my dad's office in the basement of the building where he ran a restaurant. He'd renovated it and normally worked there with other employees, so there were computers and it had WiFi, toilets and a shower. We'd also taken a fitness machine from our flat when the basement was turned into our shelter.

In the cellar we were safe from bombs, but it was really boring down there, for my parents and for me. But at least I had internet and to pass the time I flicked through TikTok videos I had saved – ideas for posts I might want to do in the future. And there was a video called "Random things in my home that just make sense …" where people showed weird stuff in their homes. So I started filming in our home, in our bomb shelter.

My parents watched me making those typical funny Italian gestures with my hands while I filmed, I chose the most Italian music I could – Che La Luna – as the backing track. My father was in a good mood, sitting at his desk in his big chair and started to imitate the hand gestures. It was funny. And my mom? My mom is always up for anything. I said: "Mom, dance a little." And she did. She grabbed a yellow plastic toolbox and danced around the bunker with it. She's great.

That's how the first video from the bunker came about. It was a mixture of boredom, my idea to do something with the TikTok trend, and have a little fun in what was a terrible situation.

People from CNN and BBC saw the video and contacted me, asking to do interviews. My city was being destroyed, but I was able to tell the world about it, and journalists had found me thanks to my TikTok from our bomb shelter.

The Escape From Ukraine

I stayed in the bomb shelter, my dad's old office, for 17 days. It had been 17 days just surviving while there was heavy fighting around us. The Russians were threatening to attack the civilians trying to get out with planes and missiles. That day, the Ukraina hotel in Chernihiv was destroyed.

We had no electricity, so people were charging their cellphones in the street from public electric points, but even then there was no phone connection. It was bad, so we decided I should leave Chernihiv, go back to Kyiv and then try to get out of Ukraine.

I thought about taking the bus to Kyiv railway station, because Russian soldiers were shooting at any civilian cars. But a couple, a man and wife, offered me a lift. So I decided to risk it and drive with them. The journey from Chernihiv to Kyiv took us seven hours – it normally takes two. Imagine a convoy of 30 cars driving in the dark across fields and through woods. Some cars had stickers saying 'Children' on them, but it didn't help: Russian soldiers will shoot anybody. Some Ukrainians had taken down the town signs to confuse the troops who were still using paper road maps. We reached Kyiv railway station after seven hours, but the journey passed quickly, because I was nervous. I was so nervous, I forgot how to pee. Even when the whole car convoy stopped to pee.

I managed to take a train to Lviv in western Ukraine, about 70 kilometres from the Polish border. On the journey, I met some other girls from Chernihiv.

I remember exactly the smell that hit me when we reached Lviv train station. It smelled of people, of food and misfortune. It's difficult to describe, it was horrible. All these people trying to get free food as well as a lot of vagrants trying to find something to eat. Suddenly I hear there is a train leaving for Przemyśl, Poland. I didn't want to wait any longer, the girls and I agreed to try to get this train.

I decided to jump the queue waiting for the train – I know it wasn't fair, but there are no rules in this game. Everyone in the line was crying and shouting, some were screaming. Suddenly, a man said there were a few standing places, so three of us got on. If we hadn't been sharp-elbowed, if we hadn't jumped the queue, we would never have left Lviv. I stood on the train almost the whole way, I could only sit down for a few moments at a time. The other girls sat near the toilet (which wasn't the most pleasant place to be). Next to me was my best friend Uliana's aunt, who was travelling with her mother who is physically disabled. It was a very sad sight.

At the station stops, people were shouting to get food. The train waited five hours in the dark at the Polish border. It was horrible – children were sleeping on the floor next to old people and disabled people. Finally we arrived in Przemyśl and I started to cry. A friend of mine was waiting for me in Warsaw – but I couldn't face another train journey.

I had no documents, and no passport as that was still in Kyiv. I thought about taking a taxi, but that would have cost $400 to get to Warsaw. So I pulled myself together and went back to the station to find a train. I decided not to wait for a train to Warsaw, but took one to Łódź, a town nearby. In Łódź I was recognised from my social posts by a local reporter and gave an interview while I waited for my friend Darina from Warsaw to pick me up. Another girl from Chernihiv was already staying with her, and now, when I think back to when I entered Darina's flat, I remember the smell of the delicious soup they had cooked for me.

At that moment, it was impossible to understand all I had been through on this journey. How was I supposed to feel?

From Poland Back to Italy

On the train from Lviv to Poland, I created an Instagram Story which I titled "Evacuation".

I wanted to tell people what it means to escape from a country that is at war. I took a lot of pictures of passengers on the train, of old frail women, of a little girl with a stuffed animal on her lap, of people screaming and of the many volunteers. These amazing people who served us as we got off the train and fed us when we arrived.

And, as part of the Evacuation Story, I wrote down some important advice:

One life hack for survive!
Please!!! EVERYONE!!!!
BE MORE IMPERTINENT

... it's what helped me get a place on the train.

I had reached Poland, I had managed to get out of Ukraine, but I didn't feel safe. I didn't feel anything. I didn't know how to react or to feel.

Because of the bomb shelter TikToks and the Instagram Stories from the train, more and more people started to follow me and message me.

One woman wrote to me on Instagram and said she wanted to help me with accommodation, but she was in New York. I wrote back and told her my plans. I said New York would be too expensive for me, and I actually wanted to go to Italy. She said she would try to help me.

The woman from New York knew someone, Celeste, who lives in Milan, and put me in touch with her. I now live with Celeste and her family. That's how I found my Italian family.

But I wasn't there yet. When I got to the airport in Warsaw, I was told I couldn't get on the plane because I had no documents. I tried to tell them I'm a refugee and that I'd travelled a long way without my passport (which was still in Kyiv).

They refused and said there would also be a problem in the Netherlands, where we would have to change planes. I couldn't fly and had to think of something else. I decided to take the bus to Milan, which was going to take 25 hours.

My journey from Poland to Italy took place overland. First I went to Berlin on a bus, where people were giving us refugees chocolate, soup and toothpaste, clothes and had set up a special table for pet food for anyone who had managed to bring dogs with them.

The journey to Milan was long, but the time passed quickly. When it's already taken you two days to get from Chernihiv to Poland, you don't even notice the 25 hours for the trip to Italy. I was glad to be on my way, looking out the window and listening to music.

🎧 Chase Atlantic – *Swim*

When I arrived in Milan, I met Celeste and her daughter Maria, a wonderful family. When I am an adult, I want to live like them. They have a beautiful flat, a wonderful relationship and their hearts are in the right place.

So now I was back in Italy. I had been here before on holiday, never dreaming that I would return here years later – as a refugee.

Map of Dreams

All my life I believed that something special, something amazing would happen to me. I knew that there was some kind of universal force, something bigger than me, let's say God.

When I was 16, our teacher at school asked us to write a letter to our future selves – to think about how we imagined our lives would be, what we hoped for. Then we all had to read our letters out loud to the rest of the class. My letter said I wanted to travel a lot, that I wanted to capture my life in beautiful photos and then post them on Instagram. And I always wanted to have a great relationship with my (then) boyfriend. I still have this letter in my room in Kyiv. I suggest that you take a paper and a pen (after you've finished reading this book) and write a message to your future self.

And you know what? It all happened pretty much the way I wanted it to. I've travelled a lot, I've posted beautiful pictures on Instagram and I have a perfect relationship with my ex-boyfriend. When the war started, he helped my parents.

Sometime later I created a 'Map of Dreams' to motivate myself every day. Together with my best friend Uliana, we had the idea one day to visualise what we wanted to achieve and do when we grew up. We started doing it on a specific day convinced that only then would everything really come true.

This map is still in my bedroom, on my table. Usually people use a table for working or studying, but not me. I use my table to collect jewelry and flowers, and for my motivation board. So every day when I wake up I can see what I dream will happen and what I want to achieve: there is a photo of a girl next to elephants, pictures of beautiful flats and hotels, of places I would like to travel to: for example Sri Lanka and of course Italy. I even put on a picture of a great car (and a few other things that I won't reveal, otherwise they might not come true).

I always wanted to make money too – one of the cartoons on my map is Scrooge McDuck, the super-rich Disney character. It's a picture of him diving into a huge pile of money. I used to watch the cartoon in the morning at breakfast with my parents and brother. I remember it like it was yesterday. But that must have been ten years ago. I still have it – the picture – but now, after the war started, I understand that money is not as important as I used to believe.

Last year, in November 2021, one guy started to reply to my Instagram Stories. He sent me photos of him surfing in Madeira, and I told him I had always wanted to go and I sent him the pictures on my Map of Dreams – and he said: "You can join me, send me a copy of your passport." I did, and, after three days, he sent me a ticket so I could fly out and meet him.

For me it was such a strange experience, but I don't regret it. It was spontaneous and sometimes you need to get out of your comfort zone. I don't necessarily think everyone should do it or repeat what I did - but this was my experience.

Rome, Italy and Milan

I was on holiday in Rome with friends at the end of last year, shortly before the Russians invaded Ukraine.

It was only two months before the war, but now it seems like a long, long time ago. A different world. I've always loved travelling – I've been to Lisbon and Paris, but most of all I love Italy.

It was my friend Anna's birthday, but none of us knew what to get her. I suggested we all go to Rome and rent a cool apartment. And we did – we had a wonderful time, we visited the Trevi Fountain, the Colosseum and the Sistine Chapel. It's a great city and a great place to take photographs.

Being in this amazing ancient city is a feeling all its own. I love the architecture and people's style. It's not like Italians and Ukrainians are so different – we have a lot in common. Italians are as laid-back as us Ukrainians, but if we're talking about work … then we're both really hard-working. The food here is simply delicious, the colours of the buildings are brilliant, as is the nature and light. I want to visit as many Italian cities as possible – I have photos of Italy on my Map of Dreams.

I don't know why I love Italy so much. It's like, if you fall in love with someone, you can't explain why you love them. It might be because they're kind or nice – it's a little strange.

I left Rome to fly to Madeira to meet Anton, the guy who I had met on Instagram and who had sent me a ticket to go surfing. It was really spontaneous.

When I got to the airport to leave Italy, I had the feeling of flying into the blue, to another island, another planet. I got off the plane in Madeira and it was as if I felt a different atmosphere, a different air, as if I was breathing in a different way. Different colours, everything was different. I felt like I could do whatever I wanted.

And you can, you know? If you want to go to New York you can do it. Or, if you don't want to, you don't do it. Everything depends on you. I am thankful for the people who gave me these possibilities and I appreciate it.

But my return to Italy, three months later, after we left Chernihiv and the war behind us, wasn't so great. That journey began with me making a post on TikTok. It was 4 March and the situation was getting worse in Ukraine.

Meanwhile, I thought back to my last visit to Italy and the wonderful time I had in Rome. In Ukraine, in Kyiv, I made a TikTok of me with a pot of noodles, dancing a bit, posing a bit, and our dog Torry jumping up because he smells the food. The caption was "Do u need a recipe?" and the text over the video says: "pov: she cooked pasta in a bomb shelter and imagined that she is in Italy." The video has been viewed more than 2.5 million times.

It was a way of saying how much I loved Italy and Italian people and how I wanted to get back there. It was not an accident. I always try to make a video with a message: not just for other people but also for me.

But now, today, I'm here living in Milan. The question is: Can I enjoy Italy as much as before? Now, since the invasion happened, I can't feel as strongly about anywhere as I could before war started.

"
We write each other
every single day. "

Flowers and Warnings

Anton always had a different take on what the Russians were intending to do. Because he had already seen the Russians invade Ukraine before.

For Anton, the invasion in February is the second war with Russia. He comes from Donetsk, a large city in eastern Ukraine with almost one million inhabitants. In 2014, after the student protests and the so-called Maidan uprising, Russia attacked Donetsk and Luhansk. At that time, hundreds of thousands had taken to the streets and demonstrated against the pro-Moscow government in Kyiv. People were killed. A little later the president fled and there were new elections, and Russia annexed Crimea. I was still a little girl at the time and really didn't understand what was going on. But Anton is seven years older than me, and he was 18 or 19 when it happened and remembers it well. That's why he could now see what was going to happen – even before it started. He was someone who had already experienced war in Ukraine. He could feel it was about to happen all over again.

When rumours began about the escalations and the possible invasion, Anton called me and asked: "Lera, what will you do if a war starts?" But I was naive, I didn't take him seriously at all and just laughed. Literally, I laughed out loud at him: "What war? Take it easy." Even when he called to say he was fleeing to Lviv with his parents, I refused to believe it. Lviv is the largest city in western Ukraine, has over 700,000 inhabitants, and isn't far from the Polish border.

He invited me to come with him to Lviv. I was torn, but eventually refused because I didn't want to leave my parents alone, and to be honest, I didn't know my own feelings towards him. So he went to Lviv alone with his parents. I remember exactly where I was when he had called me, asking him to join them. I was outside, it was raining, and the sky was blue. A few days after that phone call, the war broke out.

As someone who had already experienced one war, he felt it beforehand. He wanted to flee to Poland as quickly as possible. Unfortunately, he didn't manage to leave Ukraine – on the day he wanted to cross the border, a law was passed forbidding men between the ages of 18 and 60 to leave the country. Anton subsequently enlisted in the army and is now on guard duty at a Ukrainian military unit. We write to each other every single day.

After I fled Ukraine to Italy, Anton sent me flowers. That was really very sweet of him. I was in Rome for a talk show called "Propaganda" and he sent me a bouquet of flowers to the hotel. He is in the army and so far away – imagine the distance between Italy and Ukraine.

He had unfortunately been right about the war. He had seen what the Russians were doing in Donetsk and he knew very well they would do the same. He knew that they would invade other parts of Ukraine.

@valerisssh, Tiktok, 01.03.2022

I spent my childhood here, thank you Russia
TODAY PUTIN DESTROYED ONE OF THE OLD
BUILDINGS IN MY TOWN
It was a cinema that survived the Second World War
The cinema was damaged by a 9K720 Iskander
missile that came from Russia.
The force of the impact also blew out the windows of
neighbouring houses.

My Father, a Stubborn Mule (Like Me)

My social posts had managed to tell people about the war, to describe what was happening in Kyiv and also helped me to flee Ukraine and find a new home in Milan. But there was one person who didn't always like what I was doing, and that was my dad. He is from a generation which doesn't necessarily appreciate social media.

My father was a wealthy man in the '90s. He had a restaurant – which is where I spent every birthday, in his restaurant – and he was able to travel. He had a great life, and continues to enjoy it. In the building where he had his restaurant, he had bought the basement level and decided to use it as an office. And it's this basement which he turned into a bomb shelter when the Russians invaded. The one with computers, toilets, WiFi, a shower and fitness equipment. My dad is a great example – for me – of how to enjoy life and do whatever you want.

But ...

My dad is also *very* self-confident. But I know that he loves me and respects my opinions. I cried a lot in the shelter, his office, because it was a time of war, I was upset and we argued.

My mother says we're both stubborn as mules. And it's difficult to find any sort of compromise when you're offended. But we always made up in the end, I couldn't be angry with him for longer than a day. And it's not okay for my physical well-being when I find myself in a conflict with my relatives – I feel as if my whole body hurts inside. I feel like a squeezed lemon.

But my dad didn't want me to post videos with him in them. When I made that TikTok of the three of us I told him the video had had a million views – and I know that's a bit patronizing to him. He wanted me to take it down. He said: "I've already told you, I don't like it." But I answered "Dad, there's already a million views, I won't delete it."

I didn't take it down. I'm as stubborn as he is.

He is always worried about the family and takes very good care of us. One morning we checked the app (yes, there is an app where you can check if there is an alarm, you don't hear sirens down in a bunker) because my mother and I were thinking of going out – we really needed to go grocery shopping.

Since everything seemed safe and there was no alarm, we drove to a shop, bought a few things, went for a walk with our dog Torry. Before returning to the bomb shelter, we also visited places in Chernihiv that were badly damaged.

In the bunker I posted videos of what was happening to Ukraine – I was able to show how the Russian bombs had destroyed houses, homes and places I had played as a kid.

Living – and Leaving – Bomb Shelter Life

We went to the bomb shelter on the first day of war. There were air raid sirens wailing, so we knew bombs were on their way and we needed to find a safe place.

We drove to our shelter. Not everyone had a proper shelter, some had to hide in the upper floor of their house, for others it was a cellar.

On the first day of the war, we stayed overnight down there in the basement, in the office my dad had converted. That next morning, I went out to take photos of the long queues of people wanting to buy food. When I went out I saw tank tracks near our house. War was getting closer.

We gradually started moving things down there, like food and the things I had brought from Kyiv. On February 24, the day war broke out, I didn't believe it until the last minute. My brain couldn't process that kind of serious information.

In the evening we took down food: chocolate and canned mangos. Actually, I don't eat canned food – but after 17 days in a bunker, I'd eat anything. The other thing about living life in a bomb shelter, during a war, is that you start to live a healthier life. You could only buy oat milk, because all the supermarkets had sold out of cow´s milk.

In the evening we were watching the news and (really) we thought it would end soon. Going to the bomb shelter had been a little bit of an adventure – because I didn't realise 100% what was going on. I asked my dad if we had WiFi in the bomb shelter and he said yes (haha!). When we woke up, my mother said to me: "Let's go outside, let's go to our apartment again."

On February 25, the day after war began we woke up and my father decided he wanted his coffee. He just sits there and drinks his coffee – everything is okay for him. Like I've said, he's like that – war or no war, he must have his coffee on time. He drank his coffee, and we drove home in my mom's car.

On the way I saw tank tracks near our flat. I thought it was a joke or something. I was very happy to come home, I even filmed my emotions. It was great at home, I could take a shower. We came home, washed, ate, did everything we needed to. It had been weird for me to wash myself in my dad's 'office', but after living there a while, it began to feel more like a home.

On the night of 25 February we stayed at home, we did not sleep in the air-raid shelter. We spent the whole day at home and because there were no alarms we didn't go back to the basement. At night I went out to take photos – but we had a curfew, so we weren't allowed to go out between 6pm and 7am.

It was strange for me. I almost felt nothing, I had no feelings. We were sure it would end soon – almost that it was some kind of a joke. We thought we should wait for three days and everything would be good. But that didn't happen.

My father always used to say to me: "Tomorrow will be better." When I said I wanted to leave Chernihiv, he told me, please, go in a few days. It will be easier." So I waited. But we both knew, it was never going to get any easier to leave. He said again: "You need to wait, you need to wait."

But I left the bunker – and them – to travel to Poland on 12 March. Seventeen days after we first slept in the bomb shelter.

@valerisssh, Instagram, 07.03.2022

Every day I live with the hope that the war will end to-morrow, but everything is getting worse
I see my city being wiped out and Russian troops killing Ukrainian civilians.
It looks like the Second World War, when the fascists killed the Jews.
I feel like a Jew hiding from fascists, but I am a Ukrainian hiding in a bunker from the Russians.
The most important thing for me is Freedom but unfortunately I have to be the victim of a man who didn't play enough tank in his childhood.

The Effects of War, Hitler and Auschwitz

On the night of 3 March I remember watching a documentary about Hitler. History has always interested me. I'd been to Berlin before, visited a museum about World War II and the Holocaust Memorial, and, when I was 16 I had been to Poland, to Auschwitz. I knew what one person was capable of. But I didn't ever think it would happen to us today.

Earlier that day, I went out to see a house which was on fire – I wanted to film it. At noon I went to a place where a bomb had directly hit and from the street I could see into the destroyed flats and in one there was an oriental carpet hanging on the wall.

Exactly at that moment the bomb hit I was out making a video for TikTok. While I was filming the destroyed building and thinking about the Berlin Museum, the bomb hit near me. I didn't see it, but I heard the explosion – and I couldn't work out where it was.

While I was at the flats with the carpet on the wall, at the same time when I made a video, a bomb hit another building. I heard the alarm and I heard the bomb, but I didn't understand what the bomb had damaged. It was really loud and everything shook. I was outside, I was lucky it hadn't killed me. My dad was in the bunker while me and my mom were out. He'd read on-line about a bomb and the damaged building and he called us. He wanted us to get back to the bunker as quickly as we could.

I kept thinking about that oriental rug on the wall. It was like a relic from the past. Noth-ing has really changed in some people's flats. It seemed strange to me that even today, when we have Teslas and Elon Musk, people decorate their flats the way they used to, with a carpet on the wall. And it took a Russian bomb for me to become aware of that.

That night while I watched videos about Hit-ler, I thought that everything Putin is doing now is the same. It is 100 percent fascism. Later, my mother told me I had nightmares that night and kept screaming loudly. In my dreams I could hear the bombs going off.

Back when I been to the museum about the Second World War in Berlin, I couldn't imagine that this could ever be real life, it was like seeing what had happened on another planet. Now, standing in these completely destroyed flats, bombed and reduced to dust, I realised that it isn't a museum or history. It was my real life.

I know that sometime in the future a museum will be built in my hometown of Chernihiv, and girls and boys will visit it. They will not understand how all this could ever happen. How it really was. Our neighbours, Russia and Belarus, they drive me nuts.

"*Why are you filming?*
Delete everything, please."

The Social (Media) Impact

I check my phone all the time – it remembers everything better than I do.

All my life I have used social, and been good at it. When I was 12, I knew when to post, what to post and how to write captions. My school friends would ask me to help them with their posts. Everyone knew I was good at it, but I didn't know what to do with this skill, this passion. Now everyone tries to do it to promote businesses, but back then I didn't ever think I could have a career using this talent. And I never thought I would become known for it.

Eight years ago, when Russia invaded Crimea, Ukraine decided to boycott certain things. Russian TV channels were taken off air, we didn't listen to some Russian artists because they were not allowed to come to our country and we had to stop using Russian social platforms. Then, when Instagram released Stories, we started to use Instagram. (Everyone really liked Stories.) To message each other we used FaceTime and Instagram.

Back then, everybody was using Instagram in Chernihiv. I posted personal photos, but, when I became a photographer, I started to publish photos of my work on there as well. It became a means by which I could earn money. It was a professional platform.

I've posted things on TikTok since it started. I knew TikTok was going to be massive, because it became very popular around the time of Covid, or perhaps even before Covid. I posted a lot, regularly and, during Covid, my profile skyrocketed. When I published my first video, which was backstage at a photoshoot, it got 100,000 views. I was ecstatic because of the new followers I now had. And it went on and on – and all I had done was post this behind-the-scenes video.

When war came to Chernihiv though, it changed what I was filming and how social worked for me.

When the Russians invaded, we were all nervous. My parents realised something was wrong, but not me. I didn't understand what was happening. One day, we were driving near our house, we saw these tanks and I began to film them with my cellphone.

The soldiers stopped our car and asked: "Why are you filming? Delete everything. If you publish pictures of tanks, where they are, the Russians can check the location and bomb us."

That day, my mother and I decided to support our soldiers and make them something to eat. We made tea and I could watch a really touching scene from my window. There was a soldier and an old woman went to him with a pot of food, I don't know, soup or noodles, or hot cereals, and she gave him this to eat. The pot was really big, too much for one person, but these soldiers had been there the whole night and the whole day: they needed to eat, they needed their strength.

We spent that night at home and I filmed tanks from my window. It's frightening to hear them because the tracks and the engine make an incredibly loud noise. That evening I remember watching a film, Redoutable. It's a very cool film, a beautiful French film, with beautiful actors.

When I went to bed, it had been a day with tanks and beautiful films.

An Amazing Figure

My mom always supported me and always believed in me. When I gave the interviews on CNN and BBC about our life in the bunker, she said to my dad: "Your daughter will be famous, the whole world will know her." My mother is really important.

All my friends like my mom, they say: "Your mother is very beautiful." My mom has this weird special power because she eats and eats and doesn't get any thicker. She has an amazing figure – very small waist and big hips. She is thin and my friends are right, she's the best.

She likes cooking, she cooks really well and her meals taste delicious. She had nothing to do in the bomb shelter – she thought playing on her cellphone was boring – so she did what she loves to do most: she cooked.

She cooked pancakes. I can remember once, we couldn't find cows' milk, so we cooked pancakes with sunflower milk – a sort of vegan milk. She made salads and cooked cabbage. Before the war, she cooked the Ukrainian national dish, vareniki (they're filled dumplings cooked in salt water), and froze them. She took these vareniki from home and we heated them for ourselves in the bomb shelter.

My mom also cooks borscht very well. It's a traditional Ukrainian sour soup made with stock, vegetables and a fermented beetroot juice which gives it its red colour. Honestly? I don't like borscht, but I like its smell. When mom cooks borscht I like the smell, but I don't eat it. I think when I eat borscht I'll have bad breath because of the garlic in it. But my father and my brother, they love borscht.

I remember once visiting my grandmother's sister. It was very warm, and all the sunflowers were in bloom in the fields. Unfortunately, my grandmother has since died, but her sister is still alive. My grandmother's sister was born on the same day as me, on July 17, so she's also a Cancer. She served us homemade wine and salo, which is back bacon matured in spices and salt.

War makes you see life in a completely different way. All your problems suddenly become very small when there is war in your country. Now, it's no longer a simple life where my parents can go outside when they want – my father can't go to a cafe for a coffee every morning or go target shooting in the forest, which is like his meditation. My mother can't do the simple things in life any more – she's a really smart woman who keeps our family together, she loves gardening and growing vegetables, which she cannot do. It's really strange and I'm very afraid for them.

My favourite thing would be for my mother to come to Italy to live with me, because I feel like I could help her. But I'm not sure she would come without my dad.

" *Besides courage and bravery, it is perhaps the humour that touches deeply, as it speaks for a glimpse of normality and joy of life in the tragedy. In this way, the bleakness of an air raid shelter loses a little of its horror.* *"*

n-tv

Humour, Fame & Black Humour

I like black humour, it helps you get through absurd times.

When I was making videos for TikTok in the bomb shelter, I didn't think too much or too long about what to write or what the captions should be. I watched the news with my parents and made some comments which I thought were funny. Like a comedy show about politics. It was spontaneous.

I make jokes about sickness or death – things that are actually no laughing matter. But you need to take care, because there might be fanatics who think you're crazy. But to make fun of things with my friends? That's not a problem, they all have a great sense of humour. I do miss my friend just to have fun and laugh together. They're an inspiration for me – and our messages are a great source of funny stuff and that black humour.

People in Ukraine have quickly got used to this nightmare, these terrible conditions. If you see Ukrainians, people who've been standing in a queue for food for hours and hours, and you go to take a photo of them, they smile. People in my country, unfortunately, are accustomed to these situations. After I spent two weeks in a bomb shelter I got used to it. It's horrible and you shouldn't have to get used to it. You shouldn't get accustomed to raids or alarms or bombs. That is absurd.

It's like the bomb shelter video. There's nothing really funny about living in a bomb shelter, a converted office, not knowing what's going on outside and having to check an app to see if attacks are about to start. But for me, it was a TikTok trend that I thought would be funny … because nothing really made sense in our bomb shelter home at that stage.

It was so crazy. The click numbers went through the roof. A million views in one day, it went viral in the US and the UK. I posted it in Russian and then again with English subtitles and it did change my life.

It got more and more views every day. But really? I don't like the video at all, I don't like my face in it. I posted it for fun, but as it got more and more views, news channels, newspapers and magazines started to contact me.

In the beginning, I accepted every offer. But then I got tired from doing all these interviews – it became like a job, so I started to ask for donations for the Ukrainian army. I didn't want to do it for nothing, I wanted to get something back in return for my time.

I don't feel any different since the video made me "famous". Maybe something did happen, but I didn't notice. It is hard to understand – when you're sitting in the bomb shelter, and the video is going viral and I became well-known. I don't think I'm popular, but when people come to me on the street in Italy and in Poland and say "Hey Valeria! We know you," I get it.

I want people to see my videos because I want them to see what is actually going on. I can show more than the new channels ever can – because the situation is far worse and far more horrible than they can ever broadcast.

Ukrainian Soul, Bread and Babusya

I have a pair of earrings in the shape of a wheat-sheaf which remind me of Ukraine - because of the bread which is so important to the country.

Bread is very special to us in Ukraine – our flag represents a golden yellow wheat field under a clear blue sky. The most popular loaf made in Ukraine is a baton. What makes it special is that it is very soft, with a slight sweetness. You'll find it in every house. My parents always have a baton, there's black bread and white bread at home sometimes, but they always have a baton.

I have a friend, who, since the war started, has been making bread by hand in her village. She sends me pictures of her baking, and it's amazing to see these photos, even though I'm so far away from Ukraine, I can almost smell the bread though the pictures. But bread is only one part of our culture. When I was about 12 or 13 my father bought small houses in villages with only 30 or 40 inhabitants and renovated them. Every weekend I had to go with him to these places where there was no internet. I hated every Saturday and Sunday when I had to help my parents gardening or clean these houses. But now, when I remember those times, those teenage years when I spoke with old people, drank natural cow´s milk, helped my parents, planted potatoes, I understand it's a very Ukrainian vibe. I realise these are cultural aspects we need to keep and maintain. I love those villages where you can find babusyas (it's what we call old women or grandmothers), the dedushka (the old men), houses made of clay, the farming, the cows, pigs, geese …

Ukraine is so much more than Kyiv, the capital. Sure there is Ukrainian culture in Kyiv, but it is developing now and much more modern. But for me, Ukrainian culture is what happened, I don't know, 100 years ago. Before I was born, before my parents were born.

That's why I have a passion for old Ukrainian houses, books or traditional clothes. When I think of Ukraine, to me it's a village or a garden with vegetables. If you visit Ukraine one day, you should first spend two or three days in one of our villages to check out the nature, the lakes and rivers – and our sunflower fields are unbelievable. In the villages nobody speaks Russian, everyone speaks Surshyk, a mixture of Ukrainian and Russian. Even my father says people should stay living in villages to keep the villages alive, it's a continuation of Ukrainian culture.

I know that there are many people who escaped the war, who left but will probably never return. Even though, like me, they love our country.

My life has given me the opportunity to live in another country, Italy. And I have found many special people and interesting work here. But it's sad how it happened, how it came to this.

I don't know if or when I will go back. But what I do know is that Ukraine will win. I don't know when, but it will happen. When it does, when the invasion stops, then Ukraine will become the best destination in the world for tourists. Then I think people will come, see the country and its culture and change their minds. It will not only be known as a place where a war took place.

I lost one of these earrings on my escape to Poland. There's a picture on Instagram on the train where I still have both of them, so it must have been after that. I think it happened when I was in the shower at my girlfriend's flat. Now I wear the one all the time, it reminds me of the bread we had at home. And of the country and the culture I had to leave.

АРМИЯ РОССИИ

ИНДИВИДУАЛЬНЫЙ
РАЦИОН
ПИТАНИЯ

НЕ ДЛЯ ПРОДАЖИ!

My Friend Lena's Photo

When I was 16, I visited the concentration camp in Auschwitz Poland, where the Nazis tortured, beat, shot, gassed and starved to death 1.5 million innocent babies, children, mothers, fathers and grandparents. The Nazis were vile murderers, bloodthirsty beasts, the scum of the earth. I had seen the awful things people could do to each other, but I never thought it would happen to my friends, my family.

The same day that I published my TikTok post about my life in the bomb shelter, my friend Lena sent me a photo of a box full of food that the Russian soldiers had been carrying with them during the invasion.

Lena is a really close friend from Chernihiv. The picture had been sent to her from her mother. Her parents live in Alexandrovka, a small area in Chernihiv.

Alexandrovka had been taken over and occupied by Russian soldiers. Some of these Russian soldiers knocked on the door of Lena's parents' house and said: "We want to take a shower in your house and eat in your house and if you don't let us, we will kill you."

What else could they do? Her parents said: "Come inside."

Where Lena's parents live, the Russian soldiers do whatever they want, they just use people's homes. Her parents were so afraid when the soldiers were in the house, that they went to the bomb shelter. They wanted to get out and escape. They had to ask the soldiers twice if they could leave and on the second time they were allowed to leave.

Lena went to Israel. Many of us had to leave the country, some friends of mine are now in Germany, one in the Czech Republic and another here in Italy, but in a different part of the country.

I have one friend who stayed in Ukraine: my best friend Dima. But he can't escape because he is a man and 21 years old. Boys are not allowed to escape the war. We do stay in touch though, I contact Dima and all my other friends, to discuss things and have conversations with them.

And some days Dima and I have breakfast together over FaceTime.

I do worry about things. I want to help and try to solve problems or improve the situation. That's why I'm working with a volunteer organisation, called Palyanytsia, (www.dopomoga.cn.ua) which is based in my hometown, Chernihiv. We do everything we can.

Ukraine will win, but how many Ukrainian and Russian people need to die for this victory? How many people need to be thrown out of their homes, like Lena's parents? How many of us will be killed or forced to flee to other countries?

Please, Russia. STOP.

Maksim

The other day I called my brother, who now lives in Germany with his wife and daughter. I wanted to know how he was doing. He said: "The truth? Not very well. Has dad not called you? Maksim is dead and Yura is in the hospital." Yura is my uncle, our mom's brother, and the father of my cousin Maksim. My brother told me that Maksim had been killed by a Russian bomb and Yura was in hospital and would have to have his leg amputated.

Maksim, my cousin, was just 18 years old and, when my brother told me, I felt empty in my soul. It is horrible.

On 27 March, a loved one, Maksim, passed away. A cousin like a brother.

He was the kindest and most radiant, cheerful person in the world. It is unbelievable that the young body of an eighteen-year-old is now lying under the ground because a bomb hit the house, where he was with his father, feeding their dog. And Yura survived, but had to watch his son die. My mother loved her nephew. She saw him more than me when I lived in Kyiv and often told me he had helped her in the garden or in the house and how he was such a good boy.

These things, these calls home and remembering how Chernihiv used to be and how it is now, they do affect me. But I suppose I am a person who has always believed in myself and I always try to be very strong.

Life will never be the same again – we will never celebrate New Year or Easter together. I will never again see him in my mom's garden. He will never again write or call me, he will never again ask my mom: "When will Valeria come from Kyiv to visit us in Chernihiv?"

It took me two weeks to prepare myself to call Maksim's father and ask how he was. It was the most difficult phone call I have made in my life. He's still in hospital. When I called he was due to have an operation two days later.

He had been in the war in Afghanistan. He faced death many times, but when I called, he cried and cried. It was so hard to hear this really strong man tell me what had happened. He told me how he screamed: "Maksim, Maksim!" But he didn't answer any more. At that moment, a father understood that his son was dead.

When I spoke to my uncle, I felt the same feelings as the moment I heard the news for the first time. Yura will have that feeling every day of his life. It will never be the same again.

War has almost become a way of life, people have already got used to it. And some people make money out of it. Millions, billions have been sent to Ukraine, but I still read every day that people are asking for money to buy body armour or medicine. Where is the money? Check where you send your money – is it for charity or will it be stolen?

Everybody says Ukraine is a powerful country and invincible. They say we will survive. My question is: Why the hell should we 'survive' to have our freedom? Why should people die, why did my cousin have to die for this war, a war which solves nothing?

Nobody knows what comes after the war or when it will end. Nobody knows.

I don't condemn Russia, I don't hate the Russian people, Putin doesn't matter, I just want everything to end. And I wish my cousin was able to wake up - that I could see him again.

My Message to the World

One day I will return to Chernihiv, but it will never be the same. It will take years for life to flourish there again. Not the buildings, buildings are easy to replace, but you can't rebuild life.

The war is absurd, it is surreal, and death is happening right now and nobody can change it. People might know that there is war raging somewhere, but no-one can understand it like me – because I am Ukrainian, and I feel it.

I hope that no country, including my own, will ever have to go through this again in the future. It is strange that history repeats itself. History should be moving forward, progressing.

I want Russia and the Russian people to finally wake up. The Russians should be able to change things in their country. But, when I look at the Russian influencers on Instagram, people who are my age, they're lying about the war.

And these are millennials and Gen Z. Yeah, I think there are people who can change. People who need to change and should not lie about the war.

This war is not only Putin's war. This also affects the Russian people, who do not seem to realise what is going on or are not interested enough.

The Russian people can help end it and they should not be silent. But unfortunately, they don't actually believe that Russian soldiers are abusing, raping and killing women and children.

In Chernihiv, more than 700 people have been killed since the beginning of the war. The cemetery in our city was bombed, so now we have to bury people in the forest. We don't even have a normal place to bury bodies of our loved ones anymore. That's where Maksim is buried – there, in the forest cemetery.

People need to understand, I wake up every day thinking about what happened to my Maksim, what is happening to my parents, to my country. When I speak to my friends, when I listen to music, I can think about other things and switch off for a moment. But then I get a flashback to what is happening in Ukraine, the people being killed and the buildings which are being destroyed. And I will never forget it, it will always be part of my life.

In short?

Be brave like Ukraine
I hope you get to enjoy some delicious borscht
– like my mum makes it
Link in Bio 🇺🇦
всех цьом-бом!

@VALERISSSH (VALERIA SHASHENOK)

She was born in 2001 in Chernihiv, a city north of Kiev in northern Ukraine, where her parents still live today. Before the war, she pursued her passion as a freelance photographer. Meanwhile, one of her videos has more than 50 million TikTok views – her videos and messages go around the world.

When the attacks on Ukraine began on 24 February 2022, she documented the harrowing events that war brings on her TikTok and Instagram accounts. With images of brutal devastation, ironic commentary and a very personal perspective, her work reaches millions of people. She likes black humour a lot; it helps her get through these absurd times.

She says: "I remember the smell exactly when we reached the station. It smelled of people, of food and of unhappiness. It's hard to describe it all, it was just awful."

Valeria Shashenok fled by train to Poland, then by bus to Berlin and finally to Italy, where she now lives as a war refugee. It is important to her that everyone learns about what happened to her: "Because this war has become a terrible reality for me. It is absurd, it is surreal, and death is happening right now and no one can change it."

Your personal Map of Dreams

Your personal Map of Dreams

Hey, did you like the book – do you want to write one too?

www.story.one